Wealth With...
The Paycheck Plan

By: Hylan and Emily Harper

Do you wonder why it seems you never have enough money? Do you find yourself thinking that if you just had more money then you could do all of the things you want to do? Does it amaze you how extra income earned from working overtime, receiving a tax refund, or that birthday check Grandma sends to you every year seems to be spent before it even arrives?

If you have answered yes to the above questions, then I urge you to take control of your finances by following "The Paycheck Plan!" This plan will empower you to be able to do many of the things you want to do now like take vacations, enjoy the holidays, buy some of those must-have items, and take care of those necessary obligations like house payments, bills, and living expenses, but also prepare you for a comfortable retirement.

"The Paycheck Plan" really does work but it will require you to be disciplined! If you can commit to being disciplined, then you can achieve wealth with any income.

"The Paycheck Plan" is built on your monthly net income separated into 8 different accounts. Generally, monthly income is derived from paychecks, hence the name, "The Paycheck Plan." The underlying principle of the plan is that no matter what your net income amounts to, the distribution percentage in each of the 8 accounts stays the same. Thus, if you make more money one month, you will have more to distribute into each account.

Before I go on to explain "The Paycheck Plan" in its entirety, there is one thing you must do before anything else. Contribute at least 5% of your **GROSS** pay to a 401k or other company-sponsored retirement plan. If you do this first, and then follow "The Paycheck Plan," you will set yourself up for a worry-free, comfortable retirement.

Now, let's move on to the "meat" of the plan. As a reminder, this plan is based on your **NET** take-home pay. That means the amount of money that shows up in your bank account from direct deposit after taxes, health insurance, and 401k contributions that have already been made. From that net income, your money is distributed by percentage into 8 different categories as outlined below.

The Paycheck Plan

10% - Charitable Donations (there are others worse off than you)

10% - Saving (Emergency Money not to spend)

30% - House (Mortgage, Rent, Paint, Remodel)

10% - Investment or Debt Reduction (not debt creation)

15% - Utilities (Water, Power, Heat, Phone, Internet, TV, Gasoline, Insurance, etc.)

15% - Food and Toiletries

5% - Holidays and Vacation

5% - Spending!

For example, a net income of $3,000/month (or $36,000/year) would look like this each month:

$300 - Charitable Donations (there are others worse off than you)

$300 - Saving (Emergency Money not to spend)

$900 - House (Mortgage, Rent, Paint, Remodel)

$300 - Investment or Debt Reduction (not debt creation)

$450 - Utilities (Water, Power, Heat, Phone, Internet, TV, Gasoline, Insurance, etc.)

$450 - Food and Toiletries

$150 - Holidays and Vacation

$150 - Spending!

Looks like a great plan, right? The most difficult part is getting started! Right now, you are probably considering your net income and mortgage and how those items fit into this plan. You may also be wondering about credit cards, car payments, and piano or karate lessons for the kids. I will further explain how each of these items fit into the plan, but remember that I said this plan requires *discipline*.

You will likely have to make some changes to your spending habits to make this plan work. It may not be easy to change, but it will be worth it!

This plan works best if you have 8 separate bank accounts. That way, as soon as money comes into the main account, it gets allocated into each category/account immediately. This will help you avoid the common pitfall of unconscious spending, unrealistically thinking you will tighten the budget later, and eventually reaching for a credit card to make necessary monthly purchases. On "The Paycheck Plan," each dollar is earmarked for a specific purpose so that no dollar of yours is ever wasted!

Remember, implementing this plan requires discipline. For example, if the vacation account has $300 in it, then that's what you have to spend for vacations. If that's not enough money for you to go on the type of vacation you want, then guess what? You don't get to go on that type of vacation…yet. You must exercise a little patience and continue to save until you have enough money to cover the cost of the vacation. That may not be easy, but it will give you peace of mind to know that you have both earned your vacation and you can afford it. It's worth the wait!

Now that we understand generally how this plan works, let's discuss each category specifically.

10% - Charitable Donations

This world seems to care more about what we can get rather than what we can give. No matter how hard things are or how bad life gets, there is always someone who is worse off than you. Since you can't take anything material with you when you pass on, I highly recommend doing a little good with your money while you're still here. Whether you decide to do Christmas for a family in need, donate money to an organization you feel passionate about, or help out friends or family members during crisis, there are diverse ways to give. Consider this category carefully and give conscientiously. It will do your heart good!

10% - Saving

Let's be clear. This money is not for a shoes, purses, or candy. You are saving this money to prepare for unforeseen emergencies. An emergency is something you don't know is coming like: car repairs, medical emergencies, loss of employment, or other similar hardships. What's important is that you (and your spouse) are the ones who decide what warrants tapping into this account, so please use caution! If you use this money to buy a 70" TV, and then find yourself unemployed two months later, you will regret it!

I recommend accumulating a reserve in this account of at least 6 months of your total monthly net income. That number is based on an estimate of how long it may take someone to find a new job if there is a sudden loss of employment. For example, based on an annual net income of $36,000/year, you would want to accumulate a reserve of at least $18,000.

Once you have scrimped and saved and accumulated an at least 6 month reserve, you get to make a decision with your excess money. You can either keep adding the same 10% amount to this savings account building a bigger reserve, or you can use the excess money to pay off debt or add to your investment account.

Here is a word of caution to you: Avoid the mistake of thinking you have an extra 10% of your net income to put towards a new loan or something that requires a monthly commitment! If you have to dip into your emergency account for some unforeseen occurrence, you will need to be prepared to rebuild that account. It would be impossible to rebuild your emergency savings if you have committed your money elsewhere. So remember, build an at least 6 month net income reserve and then be prepared to rebuild this reserve whenever you have to dip into the money for an emergency.

30% - House

Get into a home you know you can afford! Your mortgage should be no more than 30% of your total monthly net income and your payment should include principal, interest, taxes and insurance. If your mortgage is less than 30% of your monthly net income, then you are in even better shape. The excess money in the account can be used to pay off the mortgage sooner or can go towards house maintenance/remodeling or even towards replacing aging appliances. This account is used for anything house-related, so if you have a mortgage that is less than 30% of your net income, you will have extra money to put towards beautifying your house.

10% - Investment or Debt Reduction

If you want to make it to and through retirement, you must contribute to this account! When it comes to investing for retirement, there are a few key points to know.

First, as mentioned before, please remember that you should already be contributing 5% of your gross income to your 401k or other employer-sponsored plan, making sure that your employer is matching that contribution. If your employer is not matching your contribution, then you should add an additional 5% of your monthly gross income to your retirement plan for a total of a 10% contribution.

Now as for this account, you will contribute 10% of your net income to this account which will be used for either self-directed investments or investments made with the help of a knowledgeable financial advisor.

If you are doing both of these things: contributing 10% of your gross income to a retirement plan and 10% of your net income to your investment account, you will set yourself up for a comfortable retirement. Let me explain this in greater detail because this is where it really gets exciting!

For simplicity, I will refer to these two investments as 20% of your net income, even though in actuality the 10% contribution from your gross income would work out to be a little more than 10% because it's based on your gross income before tax contribution.

For example, if your net income is $36,000 and you contribute at least 20% or $7200 a year, for 30 years, at a rate of return of at least 6%, you will have an estimated nest egg in excess of $603,000 when you begin retirement. Then when you start retirement you will be able to enjoy the same $36,000 a year income that you have grown accustomed to. Of course, this assumes that you leave the money you grew ($603,000) invested earning 6% and you only take income each year equal to 6% of what you have grown your nest egg to ($603,000 x 6% = $36,180 income per year).

The bottom line is that you'll be living off the same amount of income in retirement as you did while you were working, but your mortgage and debts will be paid off by then, so you will have enough or even an excess of funds to enjoy through retirement.

I recommend that you make an appointment with a professional financial advisor to help you determine the best investment allocation for you so that you can achieve a 6% rate of return or better on your investments.

Be cautious to build a conservative plan that does not include chasing after the next hot stock. Avoid risky investments that seek unrealistic long-term high rates of return. Build a plan you can stick with for at least 10 years at a time.

There is one small caveat to this section. If you are currently in debt, then the money in this account may be used to pay down the debt until it is gone.

Remember that the more money you are using to pay down debts, the less money you are using to build your retirement, so first GET OUT OF DEBT! Then build your retirement. Remember, the sooner you start investing for retirement the sooner you can retire.

15% - Utilities

Here is a list of items that would fit into this account: Cable/Satellite TV, Internet, Sewer, Water, Power, Natural Gas, Car Gasoline, Trash, City Fees, Home Owners Association, Yard Maintenance, Phone, Gym Membership, Car payments, Piano Lessons, Ballet Lessons, Karate, etc.

This part of the plan may be difficult for you. If ballet lessons don't fit in this part of the budget, you cannot afford them. If your truck payment doesn't fit, then you need a less expensive vehicle. Be disciplined! If you can't figure out where another monthly payment fits into your budget and it doesn't fit here, you can't have it right now. Make the difficult choices now so that you won't have to worry about it in the future. You can do it!

15% - Food and Toiletries

Buying groceries and other household items as well as dining out all fit into this category. Be wise in your spending habits. Preparing meals at home and limiting dining out will save a good deal of money over time! Become a savvy shopper and cook. If you are uncomfortable in the kitchen, educate yourself and learn basic cooking techniques. You may also need to watch in-store advertisements and sales, become an expert couponer, and buy nonperishable items in bulk, but whatever you do, get creative and make it work!

5% Holidays and Vacations

Most people wish they had more money to go on vacations or to buy gifts, but simply have not saved the money to do these things. Many well-intended, albeit undisciplined people, fall into the credit card/consumer debt trap each year because of this. Don't be one of them! Save your money so that you can go on vacations, buy your niece a birthday gift, or decorate for the holidays. Be wise in how you spend this money. If giving presents during Christmas time is important to you, you may not want to completely drain this account for a vacation on December 1. Remember, if you haven't saved for it, then you can't buy it.

5% Spend It!

This is your fun money and you are free to choose how to spend it! However, I strongly caution you against using the money in this account for any monthly payment like a new car or a monthly gym membership, because you will probably drive yourself crazy if have no extra spending money for those *I gotta have it* items. Be wise and have fun!

So, that's the plan. Now the choice is yours whether you will follow it. If you follow this plan, you will not only gain peace of mind in the short-term, but you will set yourself up for a comfortable and worry-free retirement. It will require discipline, but it is certainly worth your efforts.

What I would like you to remember is that each of your hard-earned dollars should be sensibly spent or saved. The things you buy should fit into one of the 8 categories, or you do not buy them. It is more sensible to live off of percentages rather than fixed dollar amounts, so that your budget can fluctuate up or down based on your income.

Listed below are three alternatives to the original plan, if you find your needs to be a little different from the percentage allocations of the original plan, but do not eliminate a category/account. As you follow "The Paycheck Plan" you'll see the value in each category and why they are separated in to 8 accounts.

In conclusion, I want you to make a plan for your next vacation, your holiday spending, or for buying that new bike you've always wanted! I want you to be able to afford the things you need and learn which of the things you want are worth waiting for. And most importantly, I want you to plan for the future, so that you can transition smoothly into retirement.

Stick to "The Paycheck Plan" and you will gain wealth with any income!

The Paycheck Plan: House and Food

10% - Charitable Donations (there are others worse off than you)

10% - Saving (Emergency Money not to spend)

35% - House (Mortgage, Rent, Paint, Remodel)

10% - Investment or Debt Reduction (not debt creation)

10% - Utilities (Water, Power, Gas, Phone, Internet, TV, Gasoline, Insurance, etc.)

20% - Food and Toiletries

2.5% - Holidays and Vacation

2.5% - Spend it!

The Paycheck Plan: Debt Reduction

10% - Charitable Donations (there are others worse off than you)

10% - Saving (Emergency Money not to spend)

25% - House (Mortgage, Rent, Paint, Remodel)

27% - Debt Reduction (not debt creation) (REMEMBER TO INVEST AGAIN ONCE DEBT BECOMES MANAGABLE)

12% - Utilities (Water, Power, Gas, Phone, Internet, TV, Gasoline, Insurance, etc.)

12% - Food and Toiletries

2% - Holidays and Vacation

2% - Spend it!

The Paycheck Plan: Early Retirement

10% - Charitable Donations (there are others worse off than you)

10% - Saving (Emergency Money not to spend)

25% - House (Mortgage, Rent, Paint, Remodel)

30% - Investment or Debt Reduction (not debt creation)

10% - Utilities (Water, Power, Gas, Phone, Internet, TV, Gasoline, Insurance, etc.)

10% - Food and Toiletries

2.5% - Holidays and Vacation

2.5% - Spend it!

NOTES:

NOTES:

NOTES:

NOTES:

NOTES:

NOTES:

NOTES:

Made in the USA
Middletown, DE
25 October 2023